Presented to :

_____

From :

_____

Date :

_____

DALE EVANS ROGERS

Christmas Is Always

Fleming H. Revell Company
Old Tappan, New Jersey

ISBN 8007-0983-7
Copyright © 1958 by Fleming H. Revell Company
All rights reserved
Library of Congress Catalog Card Number: 58-13765
Printed in the United States of America

Contents

Introduction	7
Christmas Is Always	11
The Magic of Christmas	15
Christmas in Our Hearts	21
Christmas Memories	25
A Shared Christmas	31
Giving	37
A Lesson in Love	41
God's Gifts	45
In Bethlehem	51
The First Christmas Gifts	59
Receiving	65
Like a New Tree	71
Traditions	75
The Meaning of Christmas	83
The Greatest Gift	89

To
REVEREND HARLEY WRIGHT SMITH
*with appreciation for his remarkable
ministry to God's little ones*

By Way of Introduction

WE ARE too worldly wise about Christmas, too sophisticated—and shoddy. Getting and spending in order to "give," we forget what was given us at Christmas; we have lost its deeper meaning and its joy; growing older, too many of us have not grown wiser about it, but only "adult." Christmas, we say, is for children.

Occasionally, throughout this little book, Dale Evans Rogers speaks to the children. "Christmas, my child, is always . . ." or "This, my child, is a wonderful mystery." But the children to whom she speaks are aged seven to seventy; they are youngsters and grown-ups. She speaks thus to those who have had the courage to remain young in heart, to all who understand that "Except ye . . . become as little children, ye shall not enter into the kingdom of heaven." The age of her "child" means nothing; she speaks to the hearts of all who are arrested by the mystic mystery of Christmas, who know that it is something more than a present under a tree, who would approach in childlike (not child*ish*) faith to discover its nobler, deeper spiritual meaning. She speaks to all the yearning children of God, for whom God made Christmas . . . .

If you insist that Christmas is just a day, perhaps you had better not read this book at all . . . .

But if you can understand that Christmas is always and has been always, that it is not a moment in time nor yet a date on the calendar but "a state of heart" . . . then perhaps you had better read it . . . slowly . . . again and again . . . . For here is Christmas as God meant it; here is the Incarnation that challenges the mind of man and warms and often breaks his heart, in such language and beauty as God might use in explaining it to His children . . . .

Here is Christmas, my child, perhaps as you have never heard it before, certainly as you shall never forget it . . . .

THE PUBLISHERS

Christmas Is Always

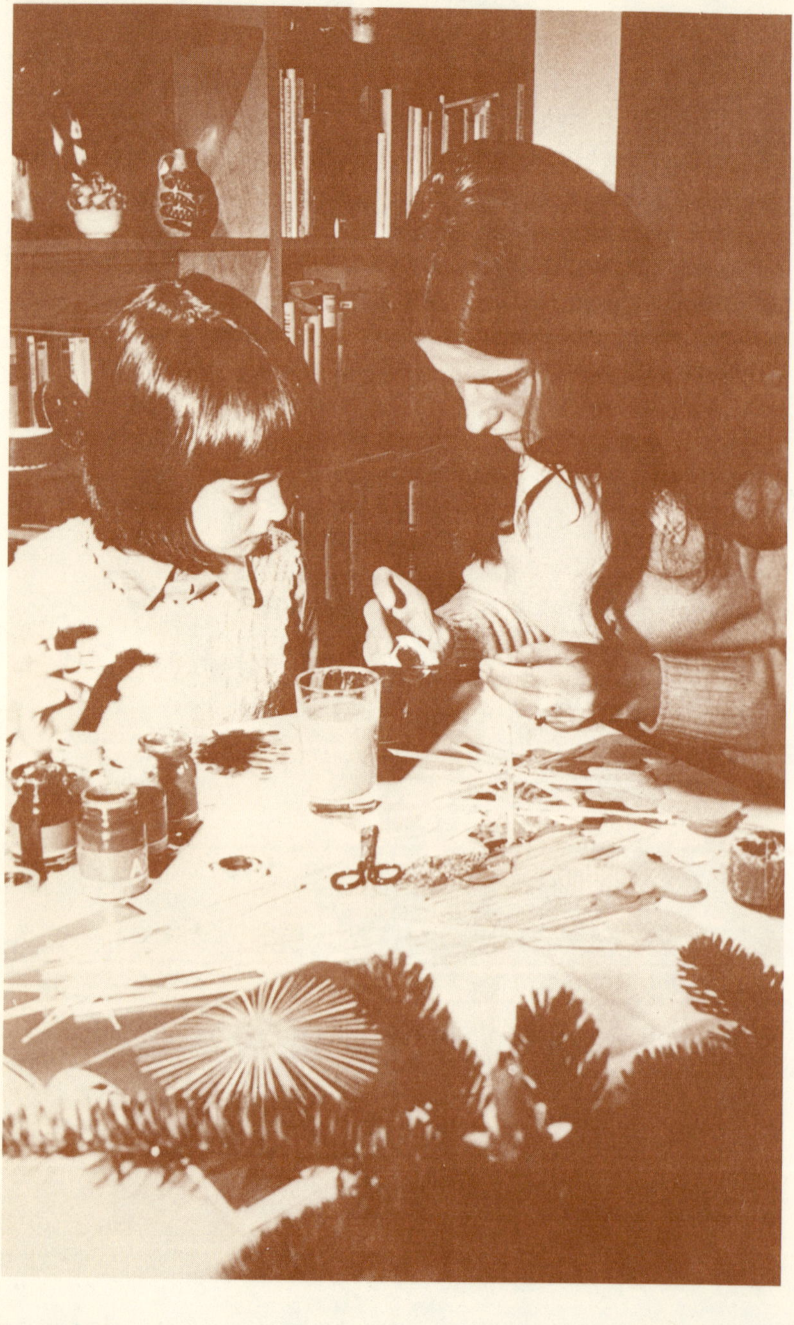

CHRISTMAS, my child, is always.

It was always in the heart of God. It was born there. Only He could have thought of it.

Like God, Christmas is timeless and eternal, from everlasting to everlasting.

It is something even more than what happened that night in starlit little Bethlehem; it has been behind the stars forever.

There was Christmas in the heart of God before the world was formed. He gave Jesus to *us,* the night the angels sang, yes—but the Bible tells us that Jesus shared a great glory with the Father long before the world was made. Jesus was always, too!

Christmas Is Always

God's Spirit has always been, too; the Spirit "moved upon the face of the waters" at the time of the beginning of the world. And the Holy Spirit visited the mother of Jesus and brought forth our Lord as the Christ Child, in the manger . . . .

Christmas is always. It has been always. But we have not always understood it.

The Magic of Christmas

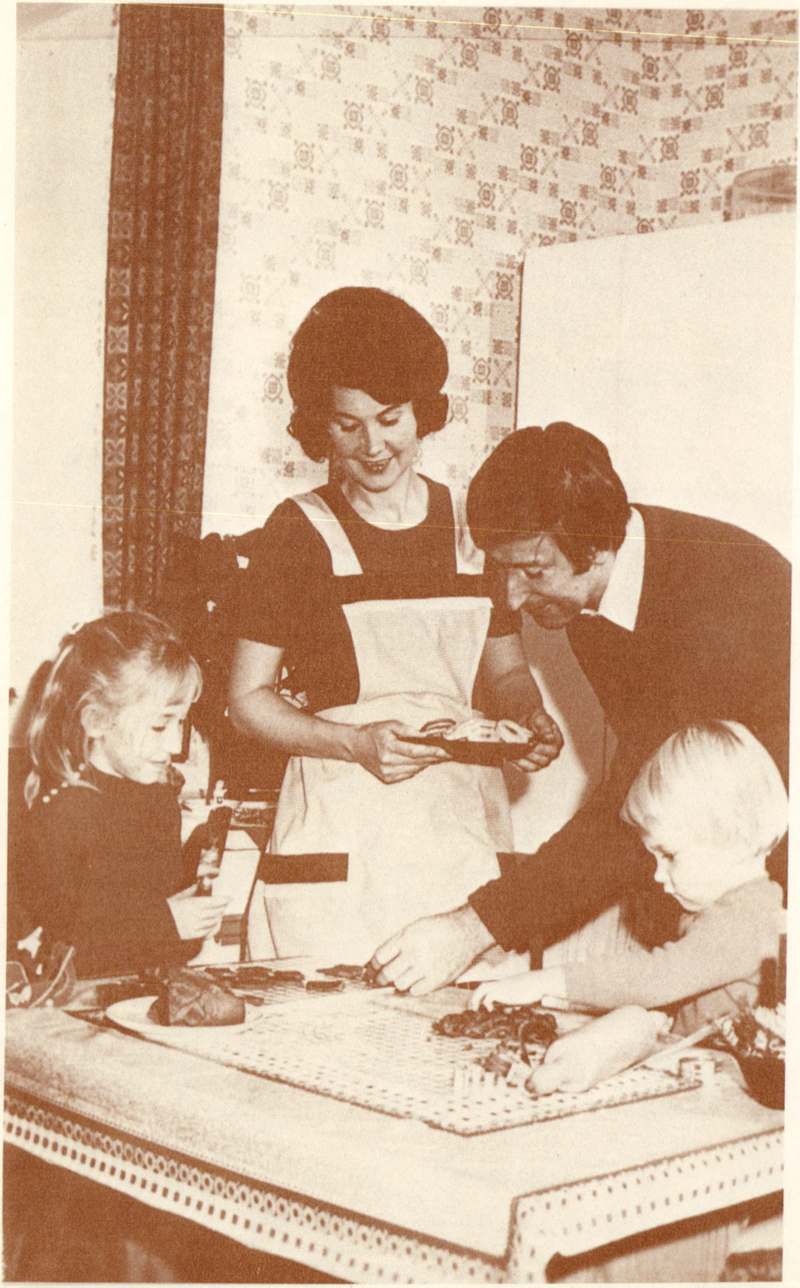

WHEN I was a little girl, the word "Christmas" was magic! It meant climbing into a railroad "sleeping car" and going from our home in Osceola, Arkansas, to my grandfather's home away down in Uvalde, Texas. It meant a happy family reunion with all my aunts and uncles and their children, under the great spreading Texas roof. It meant warm weather in the middle of winter. It meant loads of "goodies" spread on the long family table, with Grandfather at the head thanking God for His abundant blessings and asking that His grace be with us all. It meant a family gathering at an early bedtime around the huge fireplace in Grandfather's bedroom, when

Christmas Is Always

---

we popped corn and ate fresh, luscious fruit and said our good-night prayers. I can still see that blessed room, with the well-thumbed Bible beside my grandfather's big wicker chair. It was quite a family.

But, of course, we were still children then, and we spoke as children, and we understood as children, and it was a long time before we grew enough spiritually to understand Christmas as God meant it to be. (Too many of us, I think, never grow out of our childish concepts of Christmas!)

On Christmas Eve, down there in Texas, we always went to the church first, for the lovely service, and then to the town square with its breathtaking, brilliantly lighted Christmas tree, where there were little gifts for the children. And when we woke up in the morning, there was another Christmas tree which had appeared "miraculously" as we slept; the whole family gathered around it, and again we sensed the spirit of love running through the circle. There were gifts for everyone—*but not too much!* How grateful I am for that, now! The real gift was the love we had for one another, and the sheer joy of just being together, all one in love.

The Magic of Christmas

Is this not the true Christmas? Isn't that what Jesus came to accomplish—"A new commandment I give unto you, That ye love one another . . ."? At least, in those first childhood Christmases, we began to learn that lesson of love. The gifts were secondary; the greatest gift of all was the plain, simple gift of love.

Isn't it strange how children love the simple things? You can give a child a most expensive, intricately assembled toy, and after he has examined its color and mechanism, he will put that toy aside for an empty spool and a piece of string. Not long ago, a man I know complained of the way his boys "went through their Christmas gifts like a cyclone"—and by the end of the day had them strewn all through the house and all over the yard—and had turned to play with some empty cardboard boxes. He promised himself that *"Next* year they are going to get a pile of old cardboard boxes and a knife, and that's *all!"*

The challenge of simplicity is a magnet to the human spirit. Much of the beauty of Christmas lies in its challenge to look further, deeper, until we find its secret in the heart of God. But we never find that unless we look beyond the presents under the tree . . . .

Christmas in Our Hearts

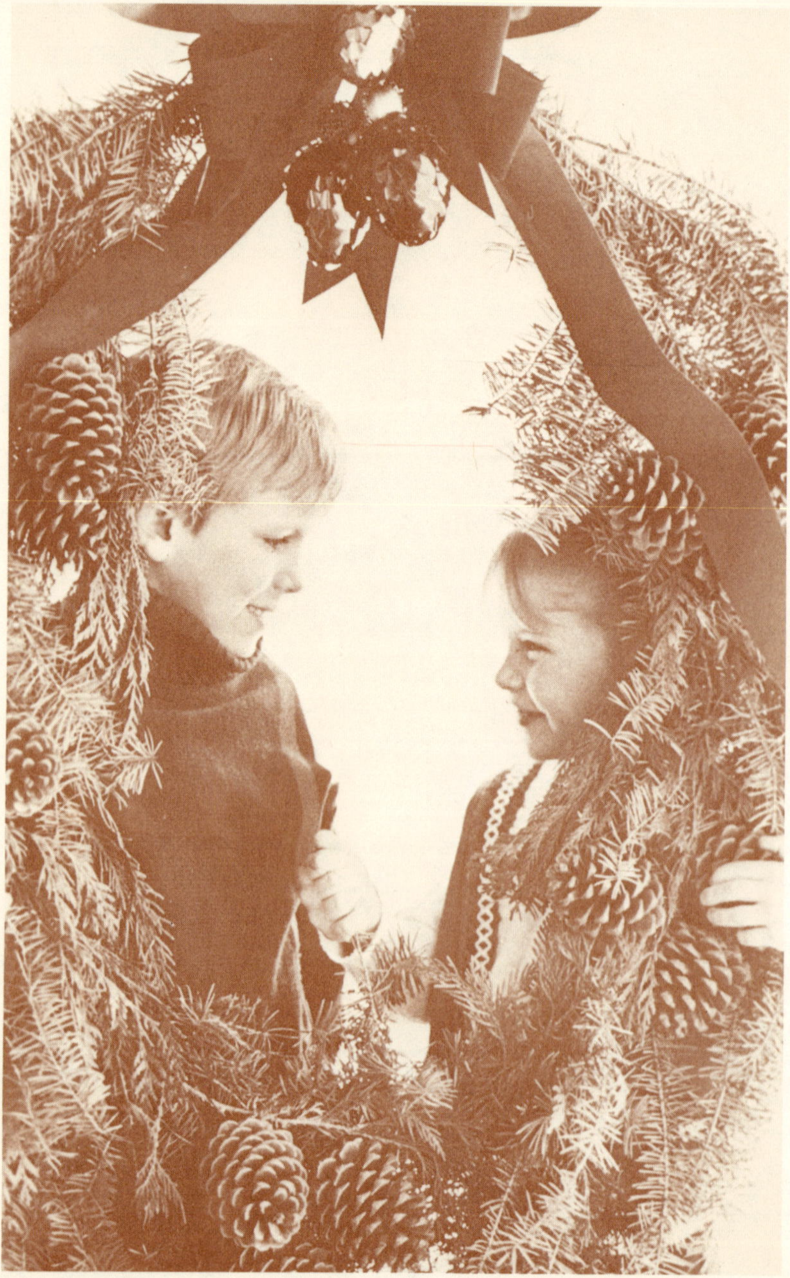

Sometimes, when I was still a child, Christmas came for me in the summer, when we visited my father's folks in Mississippi. There I found the same warmth of family love. What a wonderful time we had in that old, rambling, two-story white house in Centerville, Mississippi. There were beautiful "summer Christmas trees" on the front lawn, adorned with velvety white magnolia blossoms. I remember the heavily loaded fig tree just outside our bedroom window; I just reached out of that window, and touched it. This was Christmas, too, in our hearts, for there was an abundance of peace and love for God and each other.

Christmas Is Always

I learned that Christmas could come on a summer's day. Christmas could come at *any* season, if that sense of love were strong in the family.

Have you ever stopped to think that our Lord chose to come to earth as part of a family? He heartily approved of the family, as a social and spiritual unit. When we talk about the first Christmas, do we not always see the Holy Family in the humble manger? It couldn't be Christmas, without them there!

When we are careless about our family relationships, we are losing Christmas.

Christmas Memories

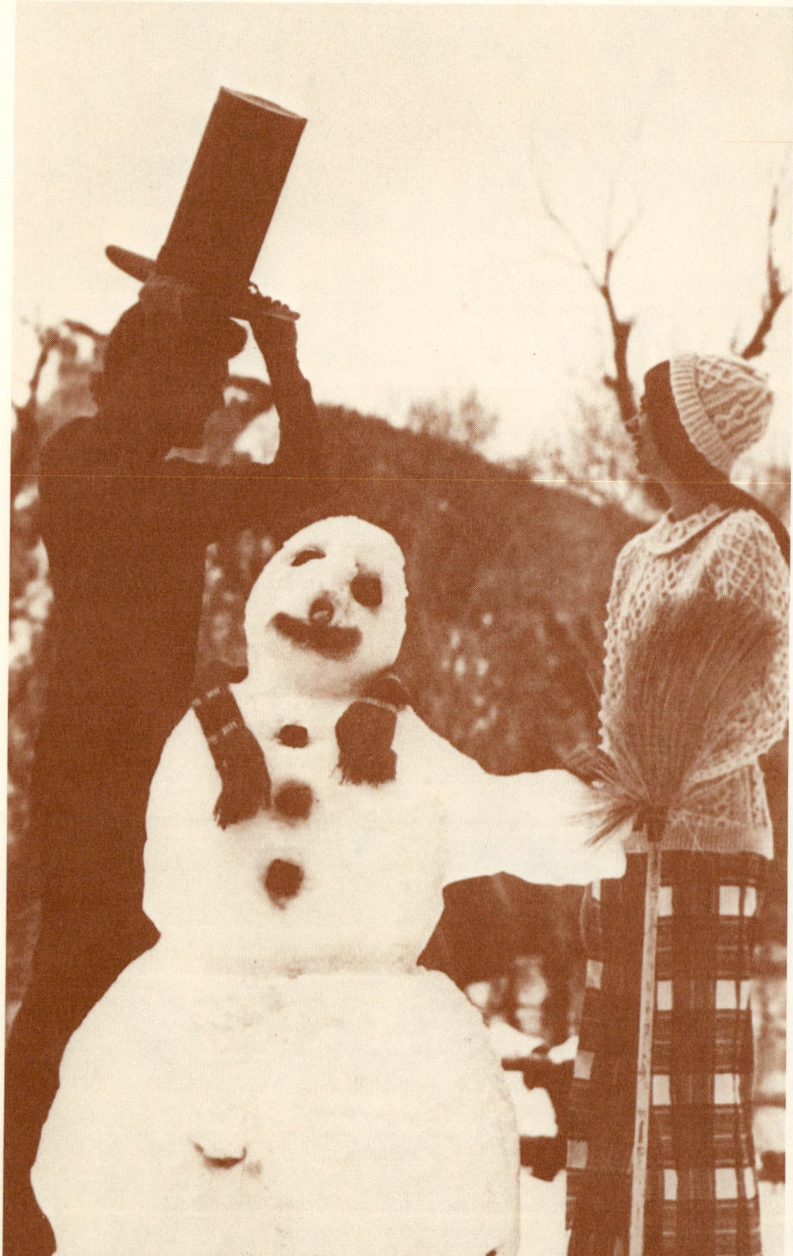

Following my marriage with my first sweetheart in my teens, God blessed me with a wonderful spiritual child, my beloved firstborn, Tom. It was Tom who gently led me to the feet of the Saviour, many years ago, by his quiet and steady devotion to Him in every area of his life. It was Roy's three motherless children and my feeling of spiritual inadequacy in meeting the problems of being a stepmother that made me look with longing at the serenity of Tom's face. I knew he had Someone he could depend upon, and I needed that Someone.

To Tom, Christmas was *every day,* for Christ was with him every day. Christ had been born *in him.* Every heart is, or can be, a manger in which the Lord is constantly reborn.

I have many wonderful Christmas memories, gathered as the years rolled by . . . . Perhaps the loveliest is the one of the second and last "earth" Christmas of Robin, our little angel. I wanted so desperately to see her enjoy, understand and really catch the spirit of Christmas, and I hoped that our carefully chosen little gifts would help and please her. You know, she looked just as though she belonged on top of a beautiful, glimmering Christmas tree. Her nurse used to call her "angel," and that Christmas day she really looked the part.

Robin was one of the greatest Christmas gifts of my life; she brought me into suffering and taught me to walk by faith with Christ through the deep waters to a new and clearer understanding of life. Through her I learned where abundant life is really to be—in the service of others through the Christ who lived, died and rose for all of us.

I remember the indescribable feeling of happiness as I watched Robin delightedly pound the little red piano that still sits on my windowsill

Christmas Memories

... and I remember hearing a song in my heart . . . .

> You little blue-eyed angel,
> Heaven has sent you to me,
> You little blue-eyed angel,
> You belong on a Christmas tree.
> Hair that is gold has my precious one,
> That little smile is warm as the sun.
> You little blue-eyed angel,
> You belong on a Christmas tree.

... what a blessed Christmas experience that was! My soul grew much in understanding that day.

A Shared Christmas

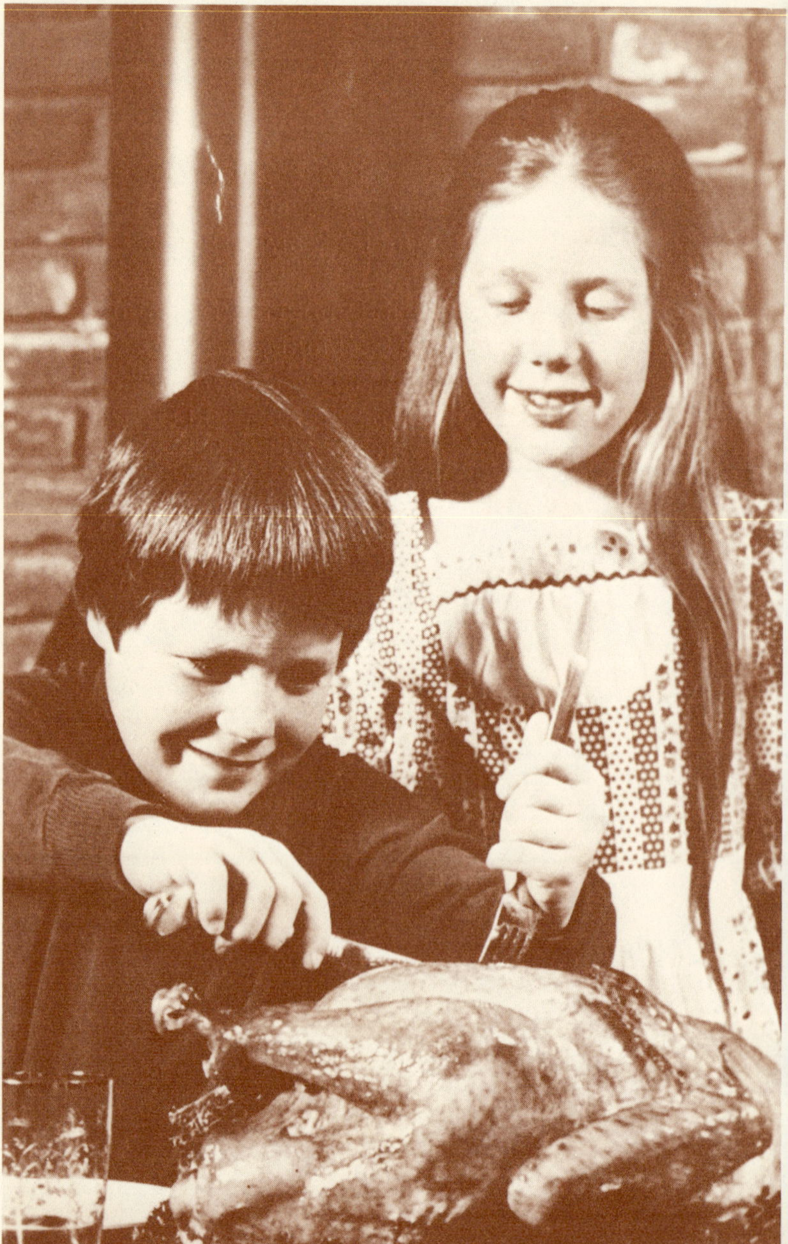

THEN, the next Christmas, as we trimmed the tree for Cheryl, Linda, Dusty and our two "newest Rogerses," Sandy and Dodie, I picked up a little Christmas-tree angel, and inwardly saw little Robin's face. As I placed it on top of the tree, I suddenly knew that little Robin was very, very happy now and having a Christmas with the One who made it possible! Sandy and Dodie were ecstatic over the tree and their gifts, and we all felt warmly grateful to God for the two charming little strangers He had sent to take the place of our "angel unaware" . . . .

There was the usual Christmas turkey with my favorite Texas corn-bread dressing, marsh-

Christmas Is Always

mallow-topped sweet potatoes, "ambrosia," and fruit cake—the Christmas dinner of my childhood. "Daddy Roy" gifted me with an electric organ on Christmas Eve, and its soothing notes proved blessed therapy to a heart remembering a little blonde head missing around the tree. It seemed the other children "outdid themselves" to help make this Christmas happy for "Mom"—because they knew I needed help . . . .

Children are "part and parcel" of Christmas . . . . Think how wonderful it would be if childless couples would "borrow" some orphans for Christmas!

The next time we had an addition to Christmas at the Double R Ranch, was when Marion, our Scottish foster daughter, spent her first Yuletide with us. I shall never forget the glow of happiness on that little face as she helped trim the tree and opened her gifts. How that child relished oranges! Oranges are so plentiful in California that we are prone to take them for granted. But I do believe that child's Yule tree was the one in our front yard, loaded with oranges!

Then came the Christmas in Chatsworth, with

A Shared Christmas

another new "little pixie" hanging ornaments on the tall tree in the den, and piping a little "sing-song" Korean rendition of "Silent Night"—little Debbie! She and Dodie wanted, and got, shiny red "trikes" and little baby dolls that cried very wee wet tears . . . .

We had nine for breakfast that Christmas morning, around the huge, round oaken table, and of course, seven of them were too excited to eat! Tom and Barbara, Mindy and Candy, Grandma Smith, and "Uncle Son," my brother Hillman, and Mammy and Grampy Slye came for dinner and rounded out the family, as well as five of our old "stand-by," or "on-the-loose" friends—so the place was really jumping with joy. You need something like that, at Christmas; you need to share it with a *crowd*. The Bethlehem stable was crowded, you know: Christ was not born in obscurity.

As I watched little Debbie chatting happily with Dodie and busy with her toys, I felt a twinge of sadness for those countless other children in Korea, and I wished I might have them all here, too. But I thanked God that day for Dr. Bob Pierce and his World Vision, Inc., which makes Christmas really Christmas for those orphans of

Christmas Is Always

the storm by providing foster parents for them in America. Yes, Christmas is always . . . it goes on, and on . . . in people like this . . . . Christmas is always.

Giving

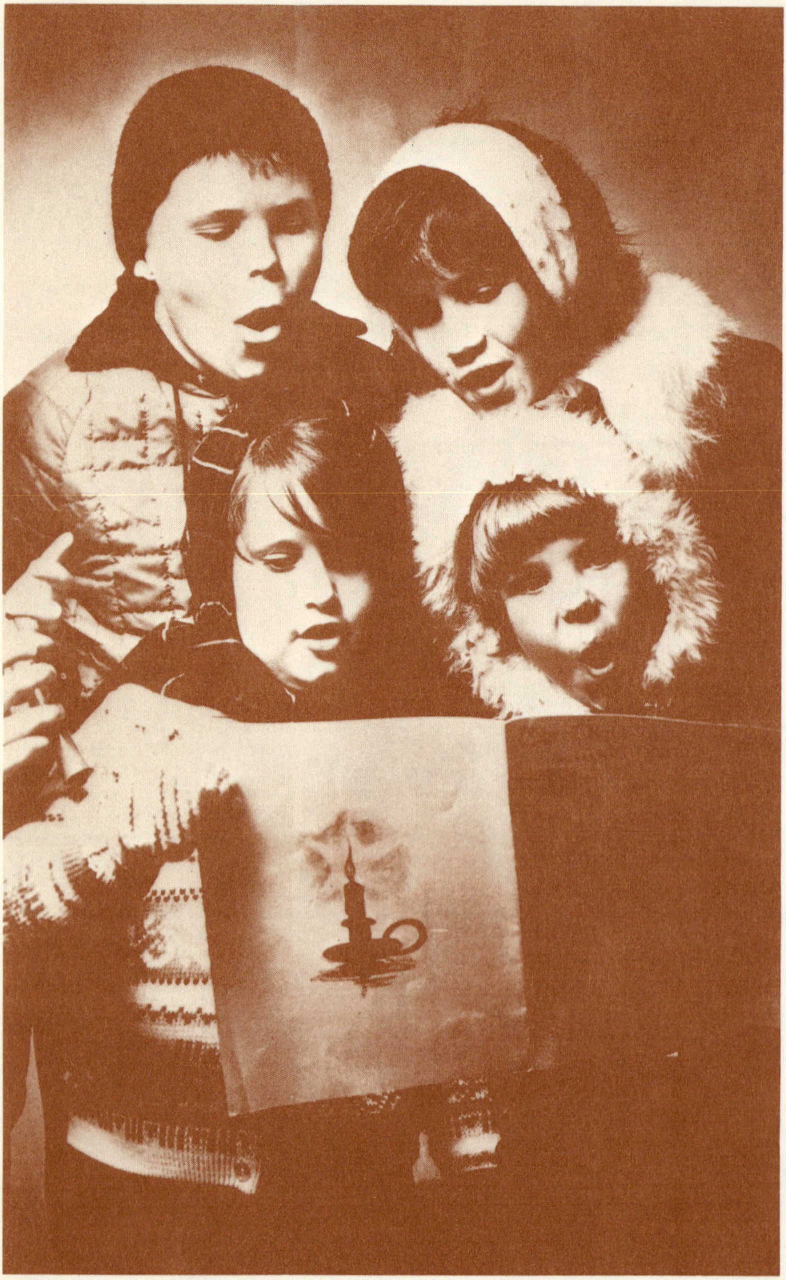

ONE day we all took a ride on the ski lift on Mount Summit, riding in pairs in the little suspended chairs which scaled the mountain. The higher we got, the colder and more beautiful it became. Our ascent was very slow in comparison with the descent of those who went down on their skis, just under the chairs in which we rode. What a parallel to life! To climb requires effort and persistence; to slide down, no effort at all . . . .

At the top we jumped out of the chairs and ran into a warm "sky house" where we drank hot chocolate and warmed our toes at the big, old-fashioned, round iron stove. The children were

Christmas Is Always

---

delighted with the little snow-covered "Christmas trees" which we saw on the way up—and there were so many! Roy said, "Wouldn't it be wonderful to have one like that for Christmas, with real snow on it?" I thought of the sixteenth verse of Psalm 147: "He giveth snow like wool: he scattereth the hoarfrost like ashes."

Giving. Always, God is *giving*. Not just on one day do His gifts arrive, but always . . . constantly . . . day by day . . . hour by hour . . . . He causes Christmas to happen with the spectacle of little snow-covered trees on mountainsides, in August and July; He trims them with a color and a glory that make our hearts leap up as we behold them. He gives unstintingly and constantly of Christmas beauty to us all, if we have but eyes to see . . . .

A Lesson in Love

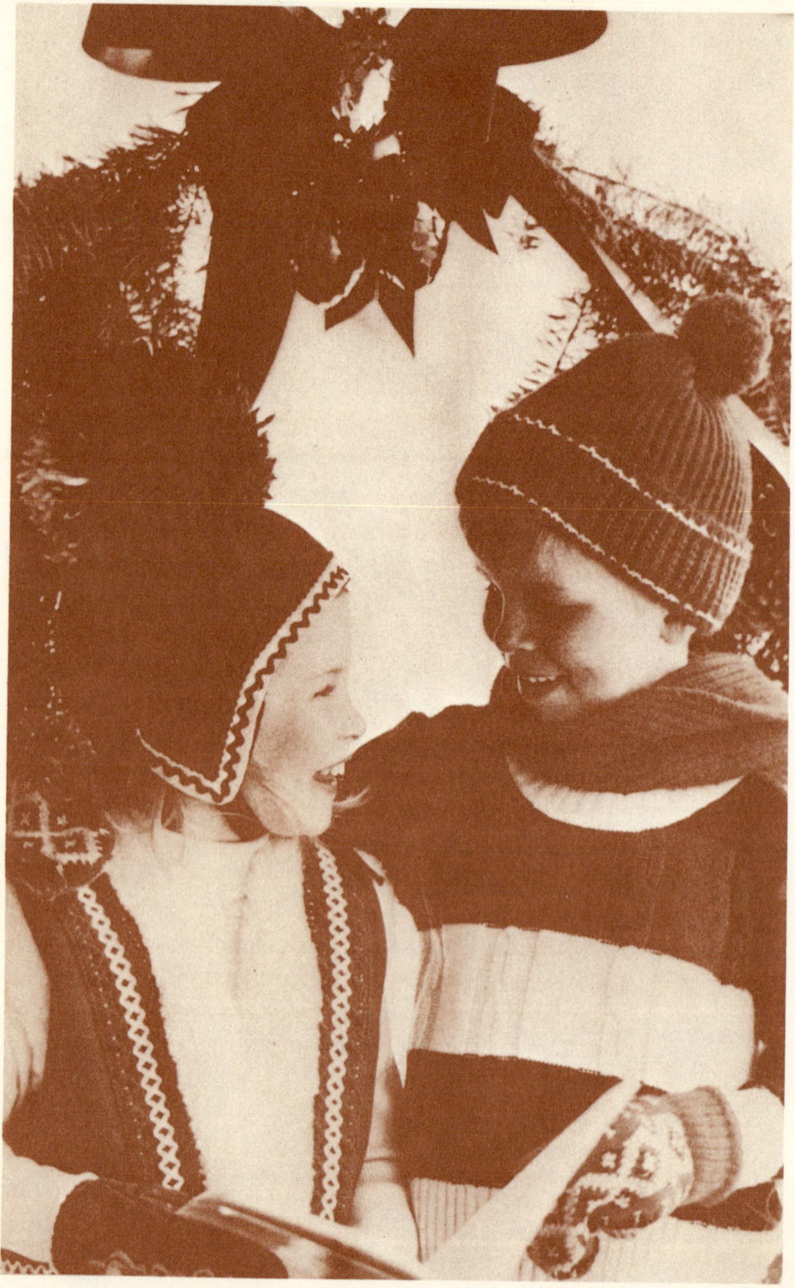

So Christmas has been for me, so it has grown and developed from my childhood days. So, I think, God intended it to be: an unfolding, growing lesson in love. And as I have grown, I have come to understand that this great love must be practiced not just on December 25, but every day in God's year.

Before me is a little story written by Robert Sylvester. It reads: "The Salvation Army always has a tough time getting the right pictures to be used for each coming Christmas and the blizzard in New York on the first day of spring this year gave them a wonderful break. The Army hurried out, found a pretty Salvation Army lassie and draped her in a red cape, broke out a stan-

Christmas Is Always

dard tripod and kettle and set it up in the snow on Fifth Avenue with the sign, 'Give a Happy Christmas.' They figured to get some good advertising and promotion pictures for next Christmas. They got them. They also got two half-dollars, four quarters, three dimes, seven nickels and three pennies—a total of $2.68—from passersby still thinking of Christmas on the first day of spring."

God's Gifts

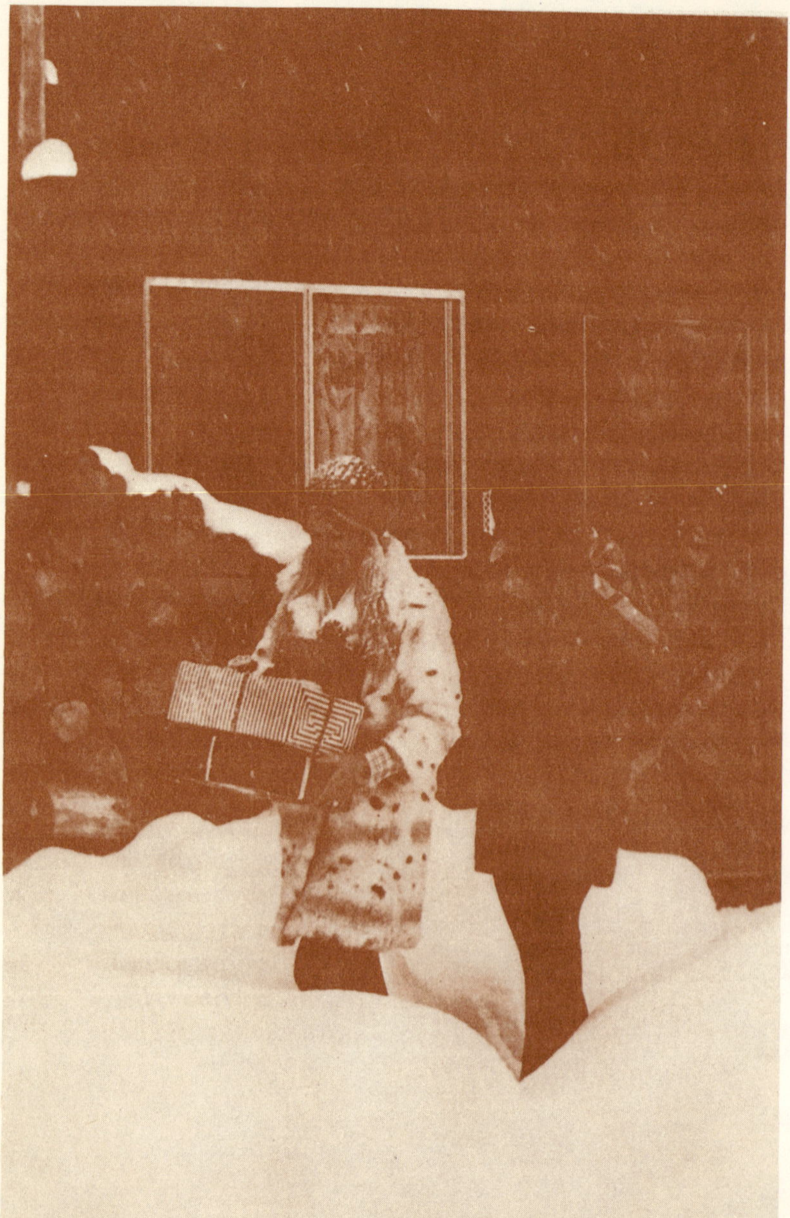

B<small>UT</small> . . . why?

Why should there be a Christmas at all? Why did God want to do all this for us, in the first place? Why? He didn't have to, you know!

You have to go back to the Bible to find the reason for it—and it isn't hard to find. This Bible was written by many men who believed in God, who prayed to God for help and understanding in their bitter, loveless world, and then listened quietly with all their minds and hearts for God to speak the truth to them. Now, God made their world and their earth with all its beauties; He was lavish with natural beauty as He finished it off, and when it was done it was perfect, and I'm sure He enjoyed looking at it. But He had some-

Christmas Is Always

thing more than beauty to lavish upon His creation: He had love to give. He wanted someone like Himself, who could talk to Him, love Him and obey Him by enjoying this beautiful world in the way that God intended him to—and, of course, since God designed it all, He knew the best way. So God made man in the pattern of Himself and then told man that he could have this whole wide, beautiful world. What a Christmas present *that* was!

The reason God made man was that man might rule the earth, for God had all of heaven and He isn't selfish. This was a *real* Christmas.

God was so loving and generous that He gave man a mind like His, to think with and to decide things for himself; He gave man the superb, priceless gift of reason, for He wanted man to search for Him and love Him because he wanted to, and not because he didn't know any better. Man's mind is the gift of God.

Then God saw that man, in his perfect earth, was lonely—because, although man could hear God, he couldn't see Him; because God, His Son and the Holy Spirit could be heard but not seen. He had formed man of the dust of the earth, so man was "of the earth, earthy." But God was not

God's Gifts

content to leave him like that. He breathed into man the breath of life, and from that moment on he was a living soul; so the spiritual side of man too is the gift of God, the eternal Giver of every good thing.

Then, seeing that man was still lonely for a mate in his earthly paradise, God made woman, so that man could be happier and so that God could enjoy them both!

Yes, Christmas is always. It was back there in Eden, with God giving, giving, giving . . . .

In Bethlehem

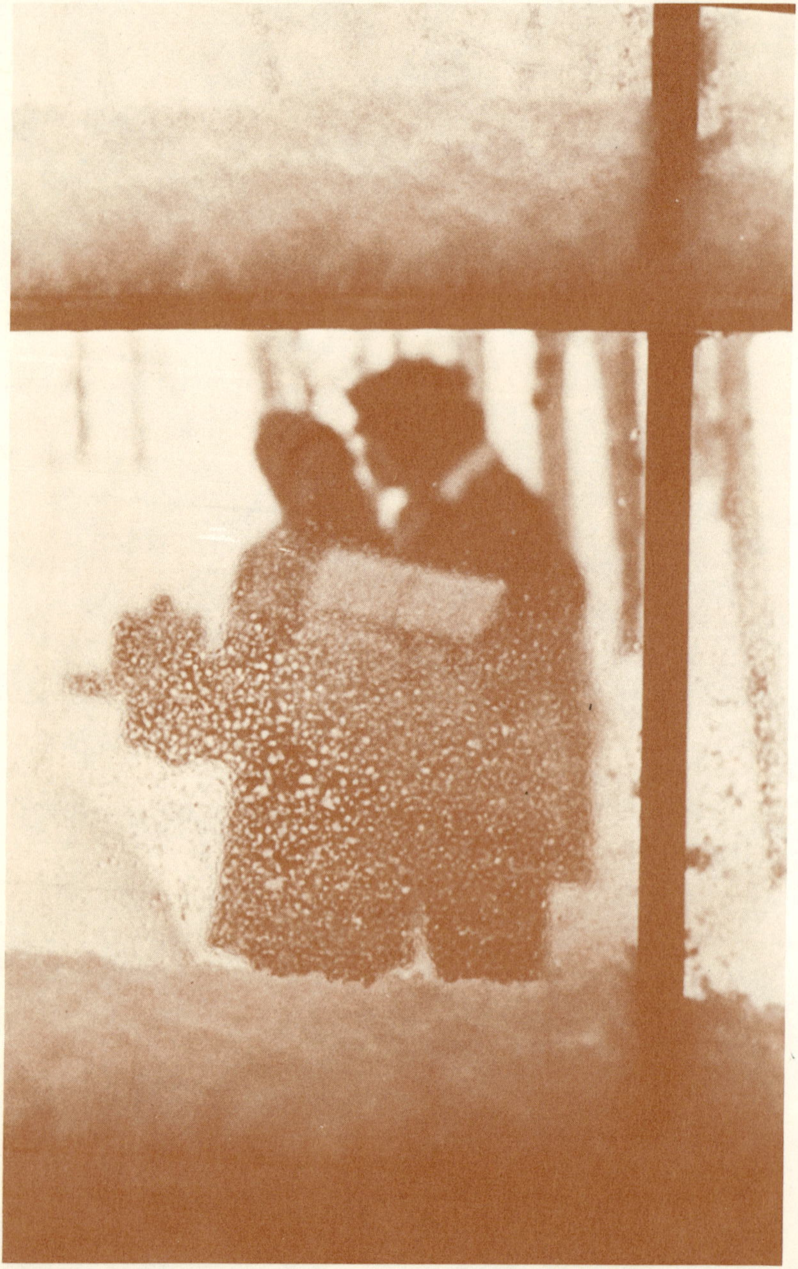

Now the man and the woman were told by God that they could eat and enjoy the fruits of any tree in the lovely Garden of Eden, except one. God knew why it would be bad for them to eat the fruit of that one tree. But the man and the woman were not as wise as God, so they disobeyed Him. When they disobeyed they were not happy and God was not happy. You all know what happened after that . . . .

The years went on, and God peopled the earth with more men and women—but they were not happy, either, because the first man and woman had brought sin, or evil, into the world, with their disobedience.

But God still loved them; He has never

Christmas Is Always

---

stopped loving us, no matter how evil we have become. From time to time, He would send certain men to earth who were filled with His Spirit, to try to get people straightened out and on the right path again. All He asked was that man love Him as He loved man. All He wanted them to do was to love each other. But, as usual, most of the people wouldn't listen to the men God sent; they were too busy having what they called "a good time." Finally, they became so wicked that God decided to clean up the world by washing it with a gigantic flood.

God is clean and holy; He wanted His people clean and holy too. He could not bear to look down upon a world grown filthy with evil. Yet, in His infinite mercy, He gave His people one more chance: He told them through Noah, His chosen spokesman, that He would spare anyone who would turn away from wrongdoing and do what was right, and worship Him. I'm sure that it grieved the heart of God that no one would listen to Noah, but no one would. So ". . . the rain descended, and the floods came . . ." until even the mountains were covered, and only Noah and his family and the animals in the ark were alive and safe.

In Bethlehem

When it was all over, God sent a beautiful present—a glorious rainbow in the sky, with colors more beautiful than any you every saw on any Christmas tree . . . .

Things began all over again, and more people came to fill the earth. In time, they forgot all about the Great Flood, and they began to abuse the beautiful, rain-washed earth again with their wickedness. God kept sending special men to speak to them, to try to get them to turn back to Him and His perfect way of life. The people treated these prophets very badly: some they ridiculed, and some they threw into prison and some they killed. They were selfish, and cruel, and they wanted their own way. The prophets were good and great men—but they failed.

Finally God was so concerned, and He loved the world so much, that He decided to try once again, with the dearest possession He had: His own Son. He would send His own Son to earth; perhaps they would listen to Him!

He knew that His Son would have to be born like a human being, and live and look like a human being, in order to reach human beings. God wanted His Son to be accepted on earth; He also wanted to show the people of earth what the

Christmas Is Always

Father, our God, is like.

God looked the world over and chose a young and pure maiden named Mary to be the mother of His Son. Now, God could have put His Son Jesus Christ on earth in any way He wanted, but wasn't it an indication of His love that He chose to honor a human being in allowing her to be the mother of His Child? What a present that was for Mary!

God decided to make the arrival of His Son startlingly different from what the world expected. So, the night of His Son's birth, He sent a heavenly host of angels to announce the birth to humble shepherds on a hillside in Judea. What a present for *them!*

The world expected the Christ to arrive in a scene of dazzling splendor, like a king from heaven. But no—God planned it otherwise. He made the scene of the nativity radiant with the simplicity of a lowly manger, with Joseph, the husband of Mary, and the shepherds, and the beasts of burden in the stalls round about. Instead of princely robes of velvet and satin, our Lord was wrapped in swaddling clothes, and He lay in a bed of straw.

You can still see the spot where He was born,

In Bethlehem

---

in a little rock-lined room cut into the hillside of Bethlehem. Thousands make their pilgrimage there every year, to stand in awestruck silence for a moment—for the greatest moment of their lives. No one ever laughs there; many weep. To no other being ever to live upon our earth is such homage paid, after 1900 years. As we go in to see the manger-spot, we pass through a little door cut so low that we must bow to get through it. No man, woman or child approaches this holy spot without a bow.

No matter which day in the week you go there, it is Christmas. Christmas is always, in Bethlehem . . . .

The First Christmas Gifts

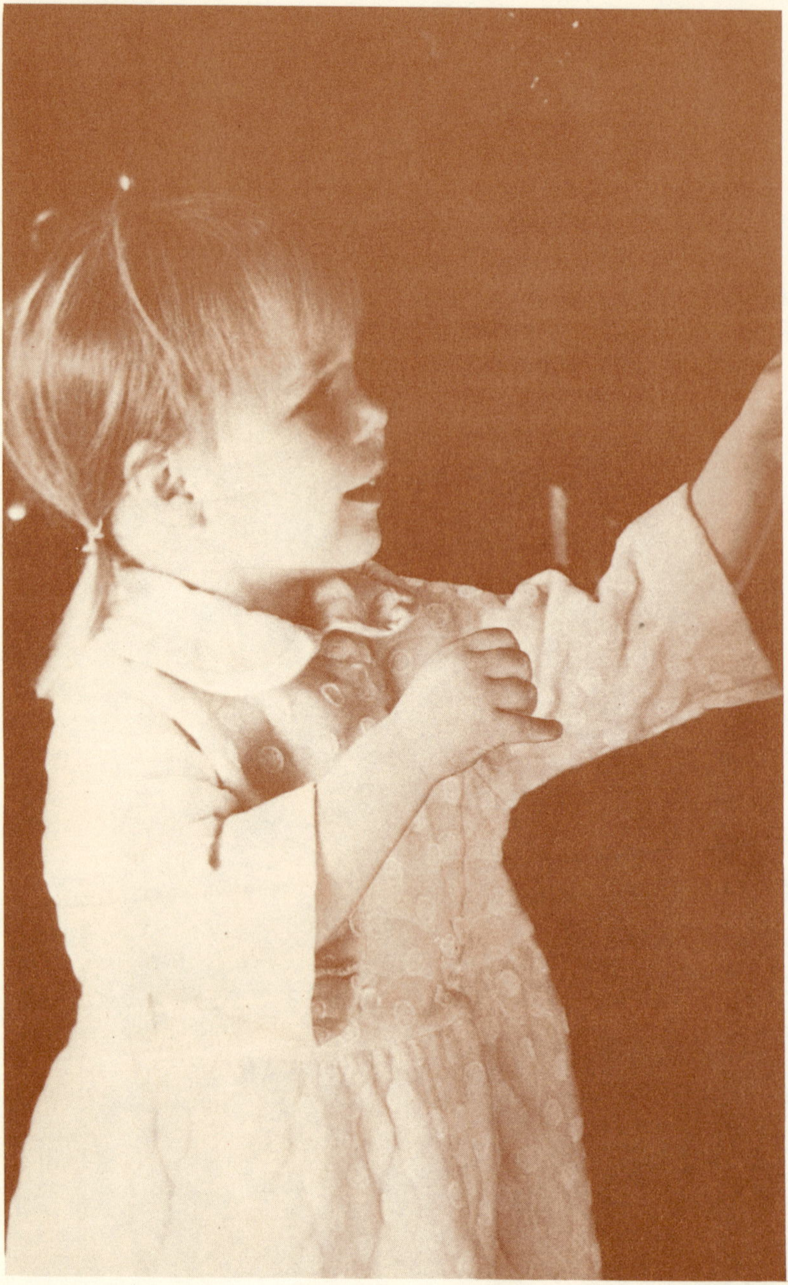

"As the heavens are higher than the earth, so are my ways higher than your ways . . ." saith the Lord. Our Saviour's coming had been predicted by the prophets centuries before, and even the kings of the Orient, far from Bethlehem, were eagerly watching for a sign of His arrival. They were so vigilant in their watchful waiting that they recognized immediately the bright new star in the East and started down the long, long road that led to Bethlehem, to see this long-awaited Messiah. Imagine their surprise when they found Him in a stable!

But perhaps it made no difference, for in the pictures we have of them standing at the manger, we see no surprise on their faces. They

Christmas Is Always

---

stand there in their rich, royal robes, or they kneel there offering their finest gifts of treasure. One offers gold; hereafter, gold is good enough only to be thrown before the feet of Jesus Christ! Another offered frankincense—a sweet-smelling incense often burned at the altars of the temple; frankincense, as well as gold is useless now; it was not holy ritual but holy living that this Christ demanded. One offered myrrh; this Babe would die young, on a cross, and Mary, happy now, would need myrrh for the embalming.

These were the first Christmas gifts from human hands to God. Study them well: they have deep meaning.

Even then, God was saying to the wise and the mighty: "Except ye . . . become as little children, ye shall not enter into the kingdom of heaven." What did God mean by giving us this Babe, by this lowly birth? Was He not giving Him as a Christmas present to the poor, and as a rebuke to those who put their trust in riches?

As He grew to manhood, Christmas was everywhere that Jesus went. He gave lovingly to friend and foe alike. He gave of His divine nature to heal the sick, to raise the dead. He changed water into wine at a wedding feast, fed

The First Christmas Gifts

---

thousands on a hillside with a few loaves and fishes, made the blind to see, forgave guilty, miserable men and women and transformed them into new, victorious people by His matchless words . . . .

Imagine the joy of Jairus, a ruler of the synagogue, brokenhearted at the death of his twelve-year-old daughter, when Jesus took the dead child by the hand and lifted her up into life again! What a Christmas for that family!

Think of what must have gone through the hearts of Mary and Martha when their brother Lazarus walked out of that tomb after four days! That was really Christmas, for, you see, Christmas is giving and Jesus really gave of His divine strength to revive those loved ones from the sleep of death.

He has been doing it ever since: millions have been lifted out of the sleep of unhappy, purposeless lives into abundant life by the gift of faith in this Christ . . . . On whatever day they accepted this gift from Him, that day is Christmas to them forever.

How much Christmas He gave! Remember the time when the mothers all crowded around Him with their little ones, and how He put His strong,

Christmas Is Always

tender hands on each of them in blessing and how His followers complained of His taking so much time for the little ones when there were so many weighty matters to be discussed, so many other more important things to be done? What did He answer? "Suffer little children . . . to come unto me: for of such is the kingdom of heaven." He was saying that Christmas is for the young in heart, and that only those with the simplicity of a child's heart can appreciate Christmas and His gifts. Those who become so wise in their own eyes that they think they need not Christ—these have lost the wonder, the true magic, the glory of Christmas.

Receiving

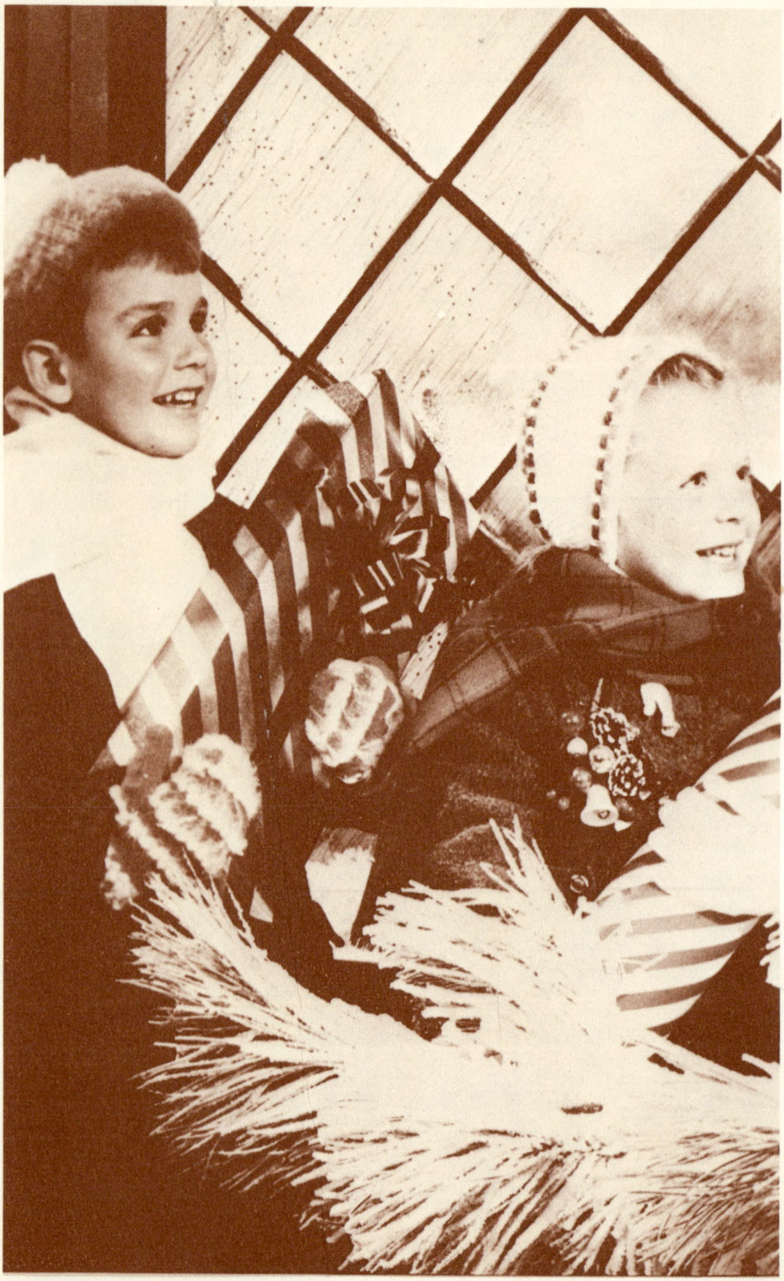

Yes, my child, Christmas is giving, in the name of Christ. But—Christmas is also *receiving!* Is that hard to understand? It shouldn't be. What would you think of the Christmas "spirit" of a friend who wasn't even grateful enough to thank you for a present? If he has the Christmas spirit at all, he will receive it with joy and gratitude and thanks, because of the love which prompted the gift. The Bible says that God so loved this world that He gave His only Son, and that "as many as receive him, to them gave he power to become the sons of God . . . ." As many as *received* Him! When we understand that, we understand that receiving is even more important than giving, at Christmas!

Christmas Is Always

Let me illustrate what I mean. Suppose a child had an overabundance of beautiful toys, and he saw a poor, ragged little fellow with no toys at all. He would feel sorry for the luckless youngster, and offer him one of the best toys he had, as a present. But—he says he doesn't want it! He still looks unhappy, when he says it. So the benevolent one picks out another, and offers that, and *that* one is rejected. He tries several times, and finally offers him his favorite toy, the one he loves best, the one he really wanted to keep forever. The other looks at it for a moment, shrugs, and turns away. This would be too bad, wouldn't it? This could have been a real Christmas for the boy, but he wouldn't receive the gift . . . .

Can you imagine how God feels when He offers us His only Son, and we reject Him, even crucify Him on a cross? You see, my child, to really receive Christmas you must receive Christ first; the rejoicing comes later . . . .

What does it mean to receive Christ? It means to understand that He came into the world to save sinners, and that we are all sinners by nature. We need to be saved from our sinful natures, or, as the Bible says, to be "born again."

Receiving

Or, if you will, "made over." When we receive Christ and take Him into our lives and let Him make those lives over, then we receive the Supreme Gift, for He comes into our hearts through His Holy Spirit and we experience the gift that is Christmas, the joy of union with God, and peace on earth and good will toward men.

Christmas is not just a date on our calendar; it is a state of heart.

The folks who have the best time on December 25 are those who have received Him, and who give in remembrance of Him. Suppose we set up a different Christmas tree this year! Suppose we set one up in our hearts. Suppose the tree is Jesus Christ, the True Evergreen, the Life Everlasting. Suppose we adorn this tree with the gifts He brings to those who accept Him—love, forgiveness, patience, hope, charity, peace, mercy, understanding, humility. Suppose we turn on the lights of this tree very brightly, and *keep* them on! If we do this, our "traditional" tree will take on a new and richer meaning.

Like a New Tree

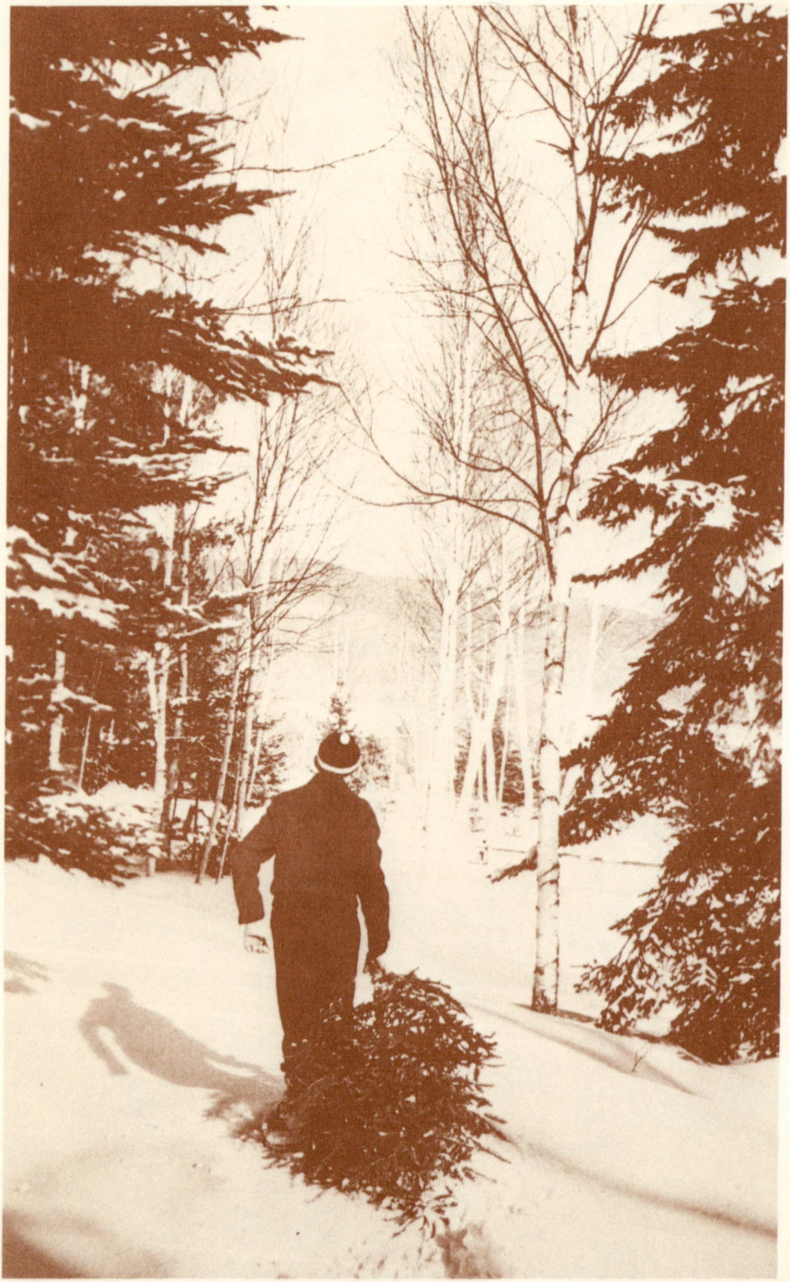

Speaking of the Christmas tree—trees, you know, have been historically recognized as symbols of everlasting life. That is, no tree ever dies: it leaves new life behind it, in seed and acorn. Job says that ". . . there is hope of a tree, if it be cut down, that it will sprout again . . ." and we are told in the first Psalm that one who loves the Lord "shall be like a tree planted by the rivers of water . . . ." It is all symbolic of the rebirth of Christ in the human heart. Every time a repentant and seeking heart says, "I believe . . ." the King and Lord of all is born anew in the humble dwelling of the heart.

The Christ Child in us must be allowed to grow, and we allow Him to grow, like an everlasting tree as we, His branches, bear fruit fit for His Kingdom.

This, my child, is a wonderful mystery, but it happens. I have seen it, and experienced it . . . .

The Bible says that the human heart is by nature deceitful, and desperately wicked. But Jesus wants His home there, so that His Spirit can change that heart. You know, when once I opened my heart to Christ in sincere faith, I was just like a little child seeing her first "Christmas tree." All of a sudden everything around me looked new and beautiful and shining . . . . I was like a new tree "planted by the rivers of water . . . ." It was the crowning Christmas of my life.

Traditions

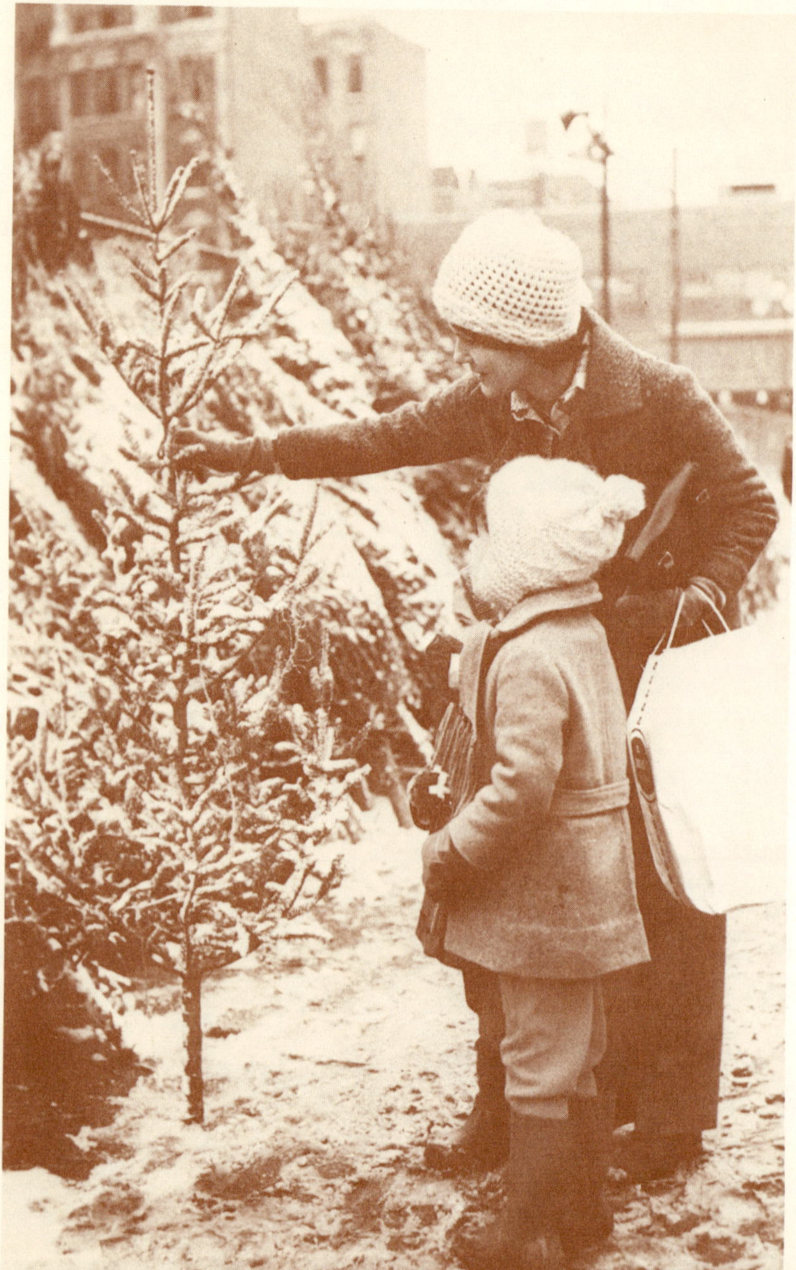

THE Christmas tree is traditional; so is Santa Claus. We've always had him around at Christmas; he's really a tradition!

But just what does Santa Claus have to do with Christmas, anyway? And how did *he* get into the picture?

Well, my child, the figure of Santa Claus is actually a symbol of the truly Christian spirit of giving, in spite of what some people say about him. He represents a man named Nicholas who, according to tradition, lived many, many years ago in Asia Minor. Nicholas' father was a very rich merchant who for years had no children. He and his wife prayed and promised God that if He would send them a child, they would train him to love and serve God. God answered their prayer and sent the boy, whom they named Nicholas.

Christmas Is Always

He was carefully and lovingly nurtured and well educated in the Christian faith.

His parents died, however, when he was quite young, and left him a great deal of money. The Spirit of the Lord prompted Nicholas to give away all he had, with the exception of three small bags of gold, which at that time would have kept him nicely for the rest of his life.

One day he overheard the weeping of a neighbor's daughter, and he heard the father say to the girl that he was too poor to give her a dowry for her marriage. (In those days a girl could not marry unless she had a dowry, or a gift of money, to bring to her husband; if she could not do this, her father had to sell her as a slave.) There were three daughters in this family, and they all wept when they were told they could not have a dowry. The girl who was at the marriageable age wept loudest of all; she was the one Nicholas heard, and he couldn't bear it. He had all three bags of his gold at this time; he crept behind a bush under the window of the neighbor's home, and tossed one of his three bags of gold through the window. He did not want them to know who did it, for he remembered the words of Jesus: "When thou doest

Traditions

alms, let not thy left hand know what thy right hand doeth: That thine alms may be in secret: and thy Father which seeth in secret himself shall reward thee openly."

So the daughter was happily married. Then came the next daughter's turn. The father was still poor, and again Nicholas heard the weeping. Again he secretly provided the dowry by tossing his second bag of gold through the window.

By this time, the father was determined to know who their "angel of charity" was—so when it came time for the third daughter to marry, he stationed a watchman outside the house, to catch his wonderful benefactor. Sure enough! As Nicholas tossed in his last bag of gold, the man grabbed him and took him in the house, where a very grateful father thanked him for insuring the futures of three tearful but very grateful girls.

Of course, this became known in the town, which embarrassed Nicholas, for he was a modest young man; and since he loved to serve God and his fellow man, he decided to become a priest. When he had finished his studies, he decided to return to his home town of Myra, in western Greece. Myra was having quite a time of

Christmas Is Always

it, right then, trying to elect a new bishop to preside in their cathedral to take the place of the old bishop who had just died. The clergy just couldn't agree on the man to fill the vacancy so they decided to wait until the next out-of-town priest walked into their cathedral, and they would make him the bishop.

While all this was going on inside the cathedral, Nicholas came along the main street of the town; just outside the cathedral he found a crowd of little children and he stopped to talk with them (and, I like to think, even *play* a little with them!). Then he stepped into the cathedral—to be welcomed by the shouts of the clergy, who then and there proclaimed him the new Bishop of Myra.

Nicholas became known as "the patron of the children" for his untiring efforts to help them and teach them. Each year on his birthday, which was December 6, Nicholas would collect presents and distribute them among the children. This idea of presents for the children spread all over Europe, and it was always done in memory of St. Nicholas, who was such an outstanding example of the Spirit of Jesus.

The word "Santa Claus" is the Dutch name for

Traditions

St. Nicholas, and we adopted "Santa Claus" when the early Dutch settlers came to New Amsterdam, or New York, as it was called later. The English called him "St. Nicholas" and, sometimes, "old Kris Kringle," but whatever they called him, they always associated him with the giving of gifts at Christmas. In the town of Myra, after Nicholas died, the practice of giving gifts continued on December 6 for a long, long time before it was finally transferred to December 25.

The red robe of Santa Claus has a religious significance too; it represents the red "cope" (or cape) which the priests of the church wore at Christmas. The fur-trimmed hat and boots were adopted by the cold countries of the north; travel there would be very cold and very difficult for Santa unless he had a sled and some fast reindeer—so he got the deer and the big sled, and he became a jolly, round, old man distributing untold happiness to children everywhere. He was never meant to overshadow the celebration of the birthday of our Lord Jesus Christ, but only to supplement it, for it was the Spirit of our Lord that gave us "St. Nicholas."

The Meaning of Christmas

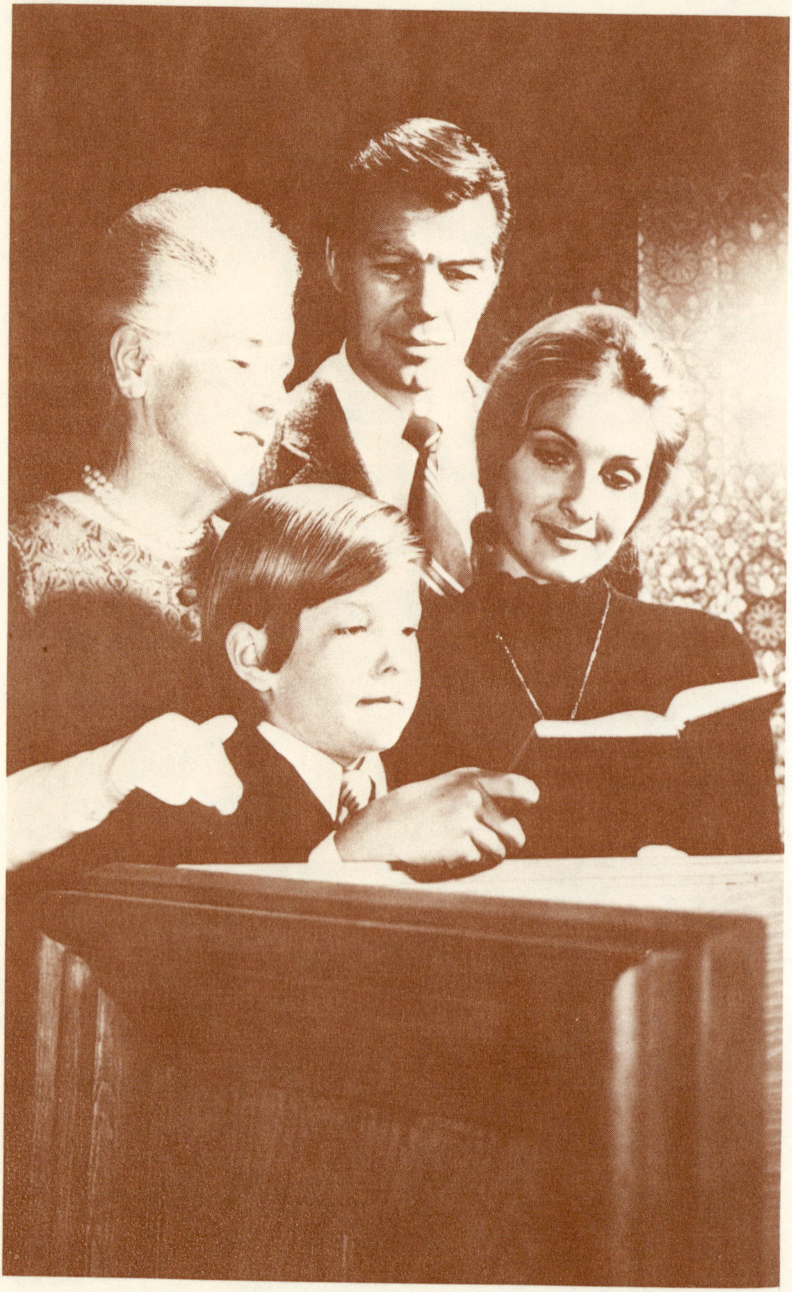

SOMEONE is asking, "If Christmas is always, as you say, then why do we set aside December 25—just one day in the year—to celebrate it?" Well, there's a lot of tradition in that, too. We might answer that question by asking, "Why do we stop work one day a week—on Sunday—instead of on Thursday or Friday?" The answer is that God gives us that one day in the week to rest, to think about what happened last week, and what will happen next week, to renew our strength through prayer and meditation so that we can face whatever comes. We *can* rest on other days, too, of course, but having a special day set aside for this seems to impress upon us

Christmas Is Always

our need for refreshment, and for the remembrance that we need to stop and "take stock of ourselves."

The same thing can be said of December 25: it is the yearly reminder that our Lord loved us enough to become one of us, to sacrifice Himself for us so that we might understand once and for all *that God is, and always was, and always will be; that God is Love, and that love will win, even on a cross.*

Love is the greatest power there is, and love is the meaning of Christmas. This is why we need a day set aside for remembering the "earth birth" of our Lord, who was Love clothed in human flesh. Christmas is the day set aside for us to ask ourselves whether we honestly love God and man. We need this day of spiritual inventory to clean out the old worthless stock of indifference and to restock our hearts and minds with the Spirit of the Christ, to receive Him and give ourselves.

Christmas, my child, is love in action . . . . When you love someone, you *give* to them, as God gives to us. The greatest gift He ever gave was the Person of His Son, sent to us in human form so that we might know what God the Father is really like! Every time we love, every time we give, it's Christmas!

The Greatest Gift

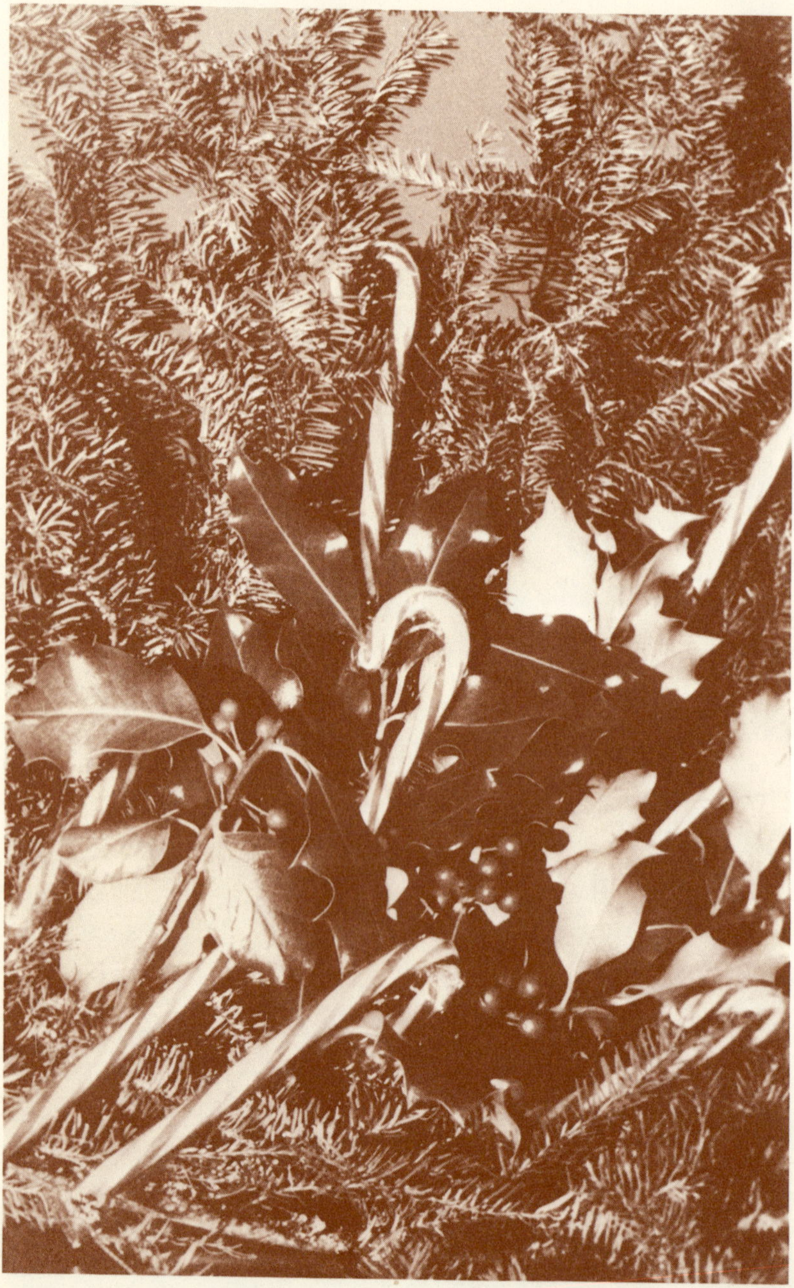

So let's put *our* love into action this Christmas.

How?

Wouldn't it be nice to visit Christ this Christmas by visiting those imprisoned by sin or sickness?

Wouldn't it be more Christlike for us to visit someone in need of food or clothes, instead of exchanging a lot of gifts and gadgets which have little use?

Somewhere on the plains of Kansas there is a humble little doctor who spreads the Christmas spirit in a chain reaction. As Christmas day comes closer and closer, the doctor writes every patient who owes him anything, canceling the bill as a sort of Christmas present! But . . . there

Christmas Is Always

is one little condition: the patient must contribute a similar amount to a worthy charity. The doctor writes the patient: "Send us their receipt and we will close your account." It is a four-way gift: from the doctor, to the patient, to the charity—and on to the unknown man or woman who benefits by it all! Why not try *that* this Christmas? Why not try a little actual forgiving of our debtors, instead of just mumbling it over in the Lord's Prayer?

Instead of worrying about what we should or should not pay for a gift for a friend, how about a donation for an orphanage in his name? You could send him a card saying that he has shared in some Christian Christmas giving with you.

How about offering Christ your talent this Christmas, instead of some of your money? He wants the best you have to give, not the cheapest! Do you know the story of "Why the Chimes Rang"? It deals with a set of church chimes that rang only when someone offered a gift that came from the heart, at Christmas. The rich gave their gold—no, gave *some* of their gold—but the chimes were silent. The not-so-rich gave "what they thought they could afford"—and the chimes

The Greatest Gift

did not ring. Finally there came a lame boy who had no money at all; he laid his crutches on the altar—and the chimes rang! I've always had an idea that that boy walked out of the church with a new strength, leaving the crutches behind.

Sacrificial giving to God always rings the bell.

How about giving up a grudge or a grievance or an imagined hurt this Christmas, to get a little peace in your heart? "Peace on earth, good will toward men!" That heavenly announcement is printed on many of our Christmas cards. Do you know, my child, that many years before the Saviour was born, a prophet named Isaiah foretold the birth of Jesus and said that He would be known as the Prince of Peace? Later, this Prince of Peace told us that peacemakers are blessed—or happy. What He meant was that unless you have peace you can never be happy. Another time, He said that if we have anything against our brother, we should be reconciled (or make peace) with him before we offer a gift to God in His place of worship.

In Czechoslovakia, I am told, the people celebrate Christmas by visiting their friends and foes and forgiving any misunderstandings which

Christmas Is Always

might have arisen during the year; Christmas to them means the ending of old quarrels and the beginning of the new year among new friends. God must love that! He never gives us His peace until we have drowned every hate and grudge and bitterness in the great sea of His love and mercy. Only when we are at peace with others do we have Christmas in our hearts.

Or, you can gather up some of the things you don't use anymore, get them to one of those organizations that mend and restore them and send them out to folks who are in need. Remember the joy each item brought you: wish the same joy to the one who receives it from you, and you will find out how blessed it is to give with such a wish. For wishes, like thoughts, are things; this way, you will be sending two things—a wish and a useful gift.

While we are at it, how about a real sacrifice this Christmas? Like choosing one of your most prized possessions, and sending it out to someone to express your love? God gave us not "something He could afford"—He gave His most precious possession in heaven, His own Son!

We need to see His Son beyond the gilt and gadgets of Christmas, need to see Him in the

The Greatest Gift

manger, in the streets, on the cross. Hilda W. Smith put it beautifully once:

> The Carpenter of Galilee
> Comes down the street again,
> In every land, in every age,
> He still is building men.
> On Christmas Eve we hear Him knock;
> He goes from door to door:
> "Are any workmen out of work?
> The Carpenter needs more."

Christmas is like that: like the walking of Jesus, like the moving of the Spirit from the days when time began to our own times, like the redemptive purpose of God working out its way in our lives through the One born at Bethlehem . . . .

Yes, my child, Christmas is always, for Jesus said, "Lo, I am with you alway . . ." and Christmas is Jesus!